THE REFORMATION MANIFESTO

Your Part in God's Plan to Change Nations Today

BY CINDY JACOBS

SAMPLE CHAPTERS

Copyright © 2007 Cindy Jacobs

Bethany House Publishers
11400 Hampshire Avenue South
Bloomington, MN 55438

Unrevised and unpublished proofs.
Please do not quote until verified with finished book.

Published ISBN 978-0-7642-0502-6
Cloth 6 x 9; 208 pages; $19.99
Available February 2008

Chapter One

Personal Reformation

I hardly felt like a reformer while standing with my friends in the afternoon's misty weather in Wittenberg, Germany. Yet, something stirred deep inside my heart as I looked at the sign on the wall that announced this museum was once the home of Martin Luther.

It was just a day or so after a conference I had done in Berlin, and our German host, Reiner, had agreed to take a few of us to do some sightseeing. As we walked down a corridor, I was a little shocked that *Lutherhalle*, the museum of Luther's life and teachings, was even open on Easter Sunday afternoon. In fact, to the people in charge of the building, it seemed like any other day rather than one that commemorated the resurrection of Jesus Christ.

Advancing through the halls of the former monastery turned home to Luther and his beloved wife, Katie, the flicker of emotion that I had sensed as I first stepped onto the ancient stone floor increased. The longer we walked and read the history of the amazing cultural changes produced by this man's life, the more my wonder grew. I kept exclaiming to our group, "Look at this!" and "Read this!" I began to wonder what was stirring inside of me. *Why was I feeling like this?*

Why indeed. You see, on those musty walls were living truths that were as relevant today as they had been five centuries ago when Luther prayed while walking these same hallways. Each time I read Luther's words my mind would bring up parallels between the need for nations to return to godliness today and Luther's reformation.

For one, Luther used the arts and music. He revolutionized church culture by writing songs that all the people could sing together in their common language. Up to that time there had not been congregational singing in church services. Worship was a key in the Reformation.

My heart caught fire as I read the lines from one of Luther's most famous hymns, "A Mighty Fortress Is Our God":

> A mighty fortress is our God,
> a bulwark never failing; . . .

Did we in our own strength confide,

our striving would be losing;
Were not the right Man on our side,
The Man of God's own choosing:
Dost ask who that may be?
Christ Jesus, it is He;
Lord Sabaoth, His Name,
From age to age the same
and He must win the battle. . . .

That word above all earthly pow'rs,
No thanks to them, abideth;
The Spirit and the gifts are ours
Thro' Him who with us sideth:
Let goods and kindred go,
This mortal life also;
The body they may kill:
God's truth abideth still,
His kingdom is forever.

Even though this hymn was written in 1529, it still touches me and thousands of others when we are in the midst of life's battles—God will prevail!

As we came to the last rooms of the museum I realized that large numbers in whole cities had been impacted by this reformation. It caused Germany to be shaken, as well as all of Europe. All of a sudden I felt like a volcano was going to erupt inside me.

Rushing out of the museum into the damp and chilly afternoon, I could no longer contain myself. With my face to the wall, tears erupted from the depths of my being as I moaned, "Oh God, I'm so sorry, I'm so sorry! My generation has utterly failed you! Oh Lord, what is wrong with us?"

You see, at that moment I had the revelation that the very elements needed to change the face of the earth had been before our eyes for centuries and yet, somehow, we have been impotent to fulfill the Great Commission.

Massive tears flowed down my face and mingled with the drops of rain as I groaned, "Eighty-two million people in Germany and only 1.6 million believers. Oh God, what is wrong with us? I'm so sorry, God. How could we have let this happen on our watch?"

At last I walked away feeling quite shaken at what I had just experienced. I knew that I had travailed deep in my soul for the nation Luther had loved—the land of the Gutenberg Bible, the first printed German translation of God's Word.

As we continued to wander the streets of Wittenberg, talking about the need for reformation fires to once again blaze in this nation and the nations of the world, we looked for the doors with the revolutionary words that Luther had penned. The famous "Ninety-five Theses" that Martin Luther nailed to the Castle Church doors are now forever immortalized with a bronze replica of the papers in the same place he originally posted them.

While we walked we talked about the problem of abortion in Germany. After East and West Germany were reunited, legalizing abortion had become a heated debate. Abortion during the first trimester had been legal in East Germany since 1972, while in West Germany it had not. A compromise was finally struck in 1995 legalizing abortion in the first trimester as long as the woman received counseling first.[1] Since that time, Germany has seen roughly 130,000 babies killed through abortion each year[2] with roughly fifteen percent of all German pregnancies ending in abortion. In the state of Berlin that percentage is about twenty-eight percent.[3] German feminists had actually rallied together, raised their voices, and marched through the streets influencing the legalization of abortion in the reunited republic.

This led to my musing, "How come the feminists have more courage than we Christians? Why is it that we aren't seeing righteous laws put into place? Why are we so weak to change things in our culture when others are bold activists passionate about their causes? Why don't *we* do something?" I queried.

"Let's pray in agreement that abortion will again be illegal in Germany," I exclaimed.

The others agreed, and we stopped to hold hands and pray on the spot. Then we continued down the same path that Luther would have taken to the cathedral.

At last, about 5:45 P.M., we found what we had been seeking—the bronze memorial on the cathedral door of the document written by the radical reformer who had shifted a whole nation with his words. We quietly joined hands and prayed that God would use us, among others, to help start a movement that would one day result in abortion being abolished in Germany. In addition we cried to the Lord for the youth of Germany to rise up and see their whole nation saved.

As we finished our prayers, the notes of "A Mighty Fortress Is Our God" resounded from the large bell tower next to the cathedral. It was as if God himself was saying, "Amen! About time that prayer was prayed. Now go do it!"

We stood in awe. The pealing of the music was so loud it shook our insides. It was a supernaturally empowered moment. However, as powerful as that hallelujah chorus type experience was, God had prepared a stronger exclamation point to our adventure that none of us could have orchestrated.

As we turned to leave, a couple who appeared to be in their early sixties was in the process of picture taking. We were surprised to see them as no one was on the streets but us. It had been messy weather most of the afternoon. This was not a typical time for tourists to be out taking pictures, especially as dusk approached.

The husband positioned his wife and I felt one of those nudgings of the Holy Spirit to go and offer to take their picture together. (I should say I was going to offer Reiner, as I knew I would probably cut their heads off in the snapshot if I took it.) The gentleman thanked us and said that his Lutheran wife had wanted her photo taken in front of the famous Wittenberg door.

After the photograph, I introduced our group—Laura, Ben, Reiner, and myself—to the couple. To our amazement he introduced himself as a pro-life lawyer from Chicago. He was on vacation from acting as counsel on cases before the US Supreme Court to overthrow abortion! We stumbled over our words as we excitedly shared with him what we had just prayed and how his being there at that moment was such a confirmation to us that one day abortion would again be illegal in Germany. After our conversation, we all prayed together and for each other.

Needless to say, we hardly needed a car to drive home as we were so excited we felt like we were flying! One day abortion will be illegal in Germany. It is comforting to know that even now God is raising up a new generation both there and across the face of the earth of radical, zealous reformers and revolutionaries who will see righteousness prevail in their nations.

Fanning the Flames of Reformation

As I have traveled around the world, I have had the opportunity to talk with people from all generations, who, although separated by age, are not separated by heart and passion. They want to be used of God to change their nations.

How does one become a reformer? If you're like some people, it's like a slow snowball, gradually gathering momentum as the need for change is clarified in your heart and you realize God wants you to do something about it. Usually there comes a catalytic moment that causes your eyes to open to the need for change. Martin Luther had one of these moments as a young man in the midst of a thunderstorm. It was a Damascus road experience for him, only he was on the road to Erfurt. It took place July 2, 1505, when Martin was twenty-one years old.

Martin was just a few miles from home when lightning struck so close to him that it knocked him off his horse. There must have been something supernatural in this wake-up call as it caused him to cry out, repenting for the sins of his youth and vowing to become a monk if his life was spared.

Martin was true to his word. On July 17, 1505, he joined an Augustinian hermitage in Erfurt—which was the most rigorous of the seven monasteries in the area—instead of returning to law school.

His father was furious at his decision because he had sacrificed to put him through school to become a lawyer. (However, Martin was going to need the skills of a lawyer when later called before the religious councils of the day!)

Martin became a priest in 1507 and began teaching at the University of Wittenberg in 1508. In 1512 he received his Doctor in Theology, but he still couldn't get away from feeling he was a miserable, unworthy sinner. In 1515 he began a series of lectures on the books of Romans and Galatians. Somehow, in the process of studying and meditating on his subject matter, God gave him a revelation that he summed up in one verse, Romans 1:17: *"The just shall live by faith."*

Regarding this experience, Martin Luther wrote:

At last meditating day and night, by the mercy of God, I . . . began to understand that the righteousness of God is that through which the righteous live by a gift of God, namely by faith. . . . Here I felt as if I were entirely born again and had entered paradise itself through the gates that had been flung open.[4]

Through this revelation, Martin Luther saw that it was not about what he did as much as about what Jesus had done. Luther experienced a personal reformation that would change his world. It was only months later that Luther nailed his "Ninety-five Theses" to the door of Castle Church.

What he had read in the book of Romans were the words of another young lawyer, the apostle Paul, who had also been dropped to his knees by a flash of light from heaven. Traveling on the road to Damascus with letters granting him the authority to bring the followers of Jesus back to Jerusalem in chains, a flash of light knocked him to the ground, and he had a similar reformation. He met Jesus face-to-face and realized his zeal was misplaced. As he later reported what was said of himself to the Galatians: "He who formerly persecuted us now preaches the faith which he once tried to destroy."[5]

The point that I want to make here is that each of us needs to have a personal reformation. Of course, the first step is inviting Jesus to forgive your sins and be the Lord of your life. However, for those who have become world-changing reformers, there also comes a moment in time—like my visit to the Luther museum—when one becomes passionately involved with wanting to right wrongs.

For many years I felt that my role in righting wrongs was entirely on a one-to-one basis. By this I mean that I would see a hungry person and feed them (which I still believe in doing on a regular basis) or pray for a hurting person. All this was good, but I wasn't engaging my mind on a macro level. My worldview needed to be refocused. I needed to reform my thinking regarding my role as a believer. My lens had been framed by the way I looked at God's commission to me personally from His Word.

My worldview began to shift in 1985 when God told me that nations could be healed.[6] Frankly, I didn't even realize they could be sick. Part of my problem was that I had been educated with a worldview based in Western/Greek thinking. The Greco-Roman—or Western—worldview is based on the individual and a separation of the supernatural from the natural.

How did this thinking affect my actions? First of all, I thought that I was only responsible to God for living a godly life rather than being a steward of my nation, its laws, and society in general. I was bound by individualistic thinking. God doesn't only think individually, but He also thinks in terms of nations and kingdoms. Biblical thinking is corporate in nature.

We can see this theme in the Old Testament in Adam and Eve's sin in the Garden initiating the fall of all humanity (Genesis 3:1–8); the sins of the ancestors effecting the generations "downline" (Exodus 20:4–6); the sin of Achan causing the military defeat at Ai (Joshua 7); the prophets of Israel condemning exploitation of the poor and social injustice (Amos 5:7–15); and the fact that Israel as a nation went into captivity. This theme is also pervasive in the New Testament from its emphasis on how we are not simply individuals, but members of the body of Christ (1 Corinthians 12) to its insistence that our responsibility extends to seeing the kingdom of God manifested in our nations.

Our worldview is critical in how we live our lives. German social economist Max Weber used terminology related to worldview in his analysis of the relationship between a people's belief system and their level of prosperity or poverty.[7] Our worldview should come through Scripture—it should be biblical. My worldview massively shifted one day when I was reading what many call the Great Commission:

> Go therefore and make disciples of all the nations, baptizing them in the name of the Father and of the Son and of the Holy Spirit, teaching them to observe all things that I have commanded you; and lo, I am with you always, even to the end of the age.
>
> Matthew 28:19–20

As I read these verses, my eyes were suddenly fixed on the words, "make disciples of all the nations." *Wait a minute!* I thought. *Doesn't that mean individuals?* All my life I had read that passage as a mandate to go out and win souls for Christ. (Please believe me, I am by no means negating the need to evangelize each individual personally.)

Grabbing my concordance, I looked up *nations* and found that the Greek word used is *ethne,* from which we get *ethnic.* The corresponding Old Testament word is *mishpachah,* most often translated "families" (as in tribes or clans). The point is that God cares about our social connectedness, our cultural backgrounds, where we come from, what our places of origin are. God also cares about how we function together in society—how our laws promote (or go against) justice and righteousness, and how we make decisions that affect all of us (politics). In Bible times, your tribe, clan, group of clans, or city-state was your "nation." However, today the main social/political organizations are *nation-states*, huge conglomerations of people brought together by social and economic forces that very often work against the tight cohesion found in tribes, clans, and city-states. Therefore, while I respect the position heralded in missions literature that the "nations" of Matthew 28:19 are strictly "ethnic groups," in this book I accept that God also meant geopolitical states and nations as they are drawn on our maps today.

With my heart thundering, I returned to my Bible and read down further, stopping at the words, "teaching them to observe all things that I have commanded." *Teaching who to do what?* I mused. And then I saw it! What I saw has reformed my worldview of my mandate as an individual on this earth. This is the revelation:

> We are called to disciple whole nations and teach them to observe everything God commanded.

My next thought after that stunning revelation was, *Is there any nation on the face of the earth where believers have been successful in seeing their whole nation discipled and their society governed by God's Word?* I know some have tried, but I could not think of one that had succeeded.

I was gripped with that thought. Christianity has been around for two thousand years. Millions of Christians have read those same words. We have the power of the Holy Spirit in our lives and yet, societies are deteriorating around us. What is the problem? How could there be roughly two billion Christians on the face of the earth today and the major problems of sin, poverty, and disease still plague the planet? Why haven't we figured out solutions to these problems? I understand that these are huge issues, but we have an even bigger God!

To be totally transparent with you, one of my major struggles in writing this book was that I wondered how I could engage ordinary believers into wanting to disciple their nations—to become reformers themselves. We will never see righteousness come to our planet without a personal reformation as to our role as Christians.

First of all, we need to care for our nations like Jesus cares for them. He loves the nations of the earth—He created them! God cares that people are hungry, that babies are being aborted. Not only that, but on the macro level, He has the answers to systemic poverty, AIDS in Africa, and other massive, mind-boggling problems. He wants to involve each of us in creating solutions and will show us what we need to do to be reformers and revolutionaries in our society.

One of the most powerful ways to learn is by looking at the lives of others who have gone before and have had a major impact on their nations.

Are You Willing to Be the Change Your World Needs?

It was 1942 in Nazi Germany. Hitler was in the midst of ravaging the youth of the nation with his lust for conquest and war. The turning point for one young woman named Sophie Scholl, a student at the University of Munich, was a sermon by the Bishop of Muenster, Clemens Galen. (This goes to show the importance of pastors being bold to cry out against injustice from their pulpits!)

Bishop Galen spoke against the emerging euthanasia policies of the Third Reich. Hitler was, with and without parental or familial permission, "euthanizing" the mentally retarded and infirm. It was in line with his Aryan eugenics plan: Hitler and his top leaders believed that the mentally ill and the developmentally delayed would contribute negatively to the "bloodlines" of Europe.[8] Over 100,000 were killed in what was called the "T-4" program. Bishop Galen declared this selective breeding "was against God's commandments, against the law of nature, and against the system of jurisprudence in Germany."[9]

Sophie and her brother, Hans, were horrified by these practices. They and some of their fellow students felt compelled to distribute Galen's sermon in pamphlet form at the University of Munich even though it was illegal to do so.

At this juncture of the war, Sophie and Hans, who had both been part of the German Youth League, had become disillusioned with Hitler and Nazism. They, along with Alexander Schmorell, banded together to write leaflets of resistance calling for the overthrow of Hitler. Hans (twenty-four) and Alexander (twenty-five) were medical students, and Sophie (twenty-one) was studying to be a nurse.

A university professor, Kurt Huber, who was forty-nine, along with three other medical students, Willi Graf, Jürgen Wittenstein, and Christoph Probst, also became involved. Together they called their group "The Society of the White Rose." The movement patterned their idea of non-violent resistance after that of Gandhi and his followers, who were fighting against racial discrimination in South Africa. Their pamphlets called for social justice as well as a return to democracy in Germany.

Most of the members of the White Rose had been in the German army and saw the atrocities done to the Jews by the Nazis firsthand. Their protest pamphlets described the mass executions and human rights violations in the concentration camps. This kind of writing was, of course, forbidden by Nazi law.

Hans Scholl had been marked to speak out against the treatment of the Jews by something that had happened during his service in the German army. His catalytic heart change from a Nazi to a reformer came when he saw a young Jewish woman who was forced to dig trenches. He thought at that moment, *There, but for the grace of God, I could have been—or one of my sisters.* Hans reached down to give her a flower and food, but she resisted. He knew that she was destined for one of the concentration camps and an almost certain death. The event so struck his heart that when he returned to medical school, he devoted his young life to his views and his faith in God.[10]

This was Hans' "road to Damascus experience." He would never be the same. Then when the gauntlet was further thrown down by Bishop Galen, he could not remain silent. History was about to be made by a handful of radical believers.

Their method at first was to write leaflets and send them anonymously to people all over Germany. They would travel to different parts of the country on the weekends and take names and addresses from telephone directories. They concentrated on university professors and bar owners—people of influence who were open to discussing new ideas.

Then came the news of the defeat of the Nazi army at Stalingrad. Hundreds of thousands of Germans were killed in that battle, most eighteen- and nineteen-year-old boys. Some 91,000 other Germans were taken as POWs—only 6,000 of which would eventually make it back home. The vast majority of these POWs died of malnutrition, disease, and lack of medical care in Russian concentration camps.[11]

I have personally stood on the mountain where the greatest fight of that battle took place with pastors from that area. The Russians were fierce fighters and their city was horribly decimated. Their losses were unimaginable, yet somehow they held back the German attack.

The news of the defeat emboldened the seven leaders of the White Rose to believe that the time to end the war was upon them. On the nights of

February 4, 8, and 15, 1943, the group painted anti-Nazi slogans at twenty-nine different sites in Munich. They wrote "Down with Hitler!" "Hitler the Mass Murderer!" and *"Freiheit! Freiheit! Freiheit!"* (Freedom! Freedom! Freedom!) Their signboards were the sides of buildings where they drew crossed-out swastikas.

They earnestly believed the youth of Germany could overthrow the evil regime Hitler had built. They produced about 9,000 copies of their sixth leaflet entitled *Fellow Fighters in the Resistance*—which this time had been drafted by Professor Huber—and sent it out on February 16 and 18. It read:

> Shaken and broken, our people behold the loss of the men of Stalingrad. Three hundred and thirty thousand German men have been senselessly and irresponsibly driven to death and destruction by the inspired strategy of our World War I Private First Class [referring to Hitler]. . . .
>
> The name of Germany is dishonored for all time if German youth do not finally rise, take revenge, smash its tormentors. Students! The German people look to us.[12]

All these actions put the Gestapo into a frenzy without a clue to who the culprits were. They could not figure out how this resistance could be thriving. Finally, Hans and Sophie were caught throwing tracts off of a third floor balcony at the University of Munich.

After their arrest, the Nazis moved with stunning speed against the three initially arrested: Sophie Scholl, her brother, Hans, and Christoph Probst. They were arrested on February 18, 1943. Just four days later, they were put on trial for treason. After the justice, Roland Freisler, ranted and raved at them, it was clear that he could never conceive how children who grew up in nice German homes could have committed what he felt were such atrocities against the Third Reich and the Fatherland.

Sophie Scholl shocked everyone in the courtroom when she answered to Freisler, "Somebody, after all, had to make a start. What we wrote and said is also believed by many others. They just don't dare express themselves as we did." Later in the proceedings, she told him, "You know the war is lost. Why don't you have the courage to face it?"[13]

Robert and Magdalene Scholl, Sophie and Hans' father and mother, tried to come to their children's defense. Magdalene tried to enter the courtroom, telling the guard, "But I'm the mother of the accused." The guard responded, "You should have brought them up better," and refused her entrance. Robert Scholl forced his way into the courtroom and, as the guards held him, he told the court he had come to defend Hans and Sophie. The judge had him thrown out, but not before the entire courtroom heard him shout, "One day there will be another kind of justice! . . . One day they will go down in history!"[14]

I cannot conceive of the pain these parents were going through. At this moment I am thinking of my own two children—now in their thirties—trying to put myself in these parents' place—oh the anguish!

The court pronounced the judgment: death by guillotine. The sentence was carried out that very afternoon.

While they waited for execution in Stadelheim prison, the guard allowed Sophie and Hans to see their parents one last time. They were both brave and conveyed their affection as well as their conviction. Hans asked his parents to give his regards to his friends, whom he named. For a moment he broke, but then faced them with a smile.

Sophie's last visit was so poignant that I want to give you the written account from *A Noble Treason* by Richard Hanser:

> Then a woman prison guard brought in Sophie.
>
> She was wearing her everyday clothes, a rather bulky crocheted jacket and a blue skirt, and she was smiling. Her mother tentatively offered her some candy, which Hans had declined.
>
> "Gladly," said Sophie, taking it. "After all, I haven't had any lunch!"
> She, too, looked somehow smaller, as if drawn together, but her face was clear and her smile was fresh and unforced, with something in it that her parents read as triumph.
>
> "Sophie, Sophie," her mother murmured, as if to herself. "To think you'll never be coming through the door again!" Sophie's smile was gentle.
>
> "Ah Mother," she said, "Those few little years . . ."
>
> Sophie Scholl looked at her parents and was strong in her pride and certainty. "We took everything upon ourselves," she said. "What we did will cause waves."
>
> Her mother spoke again: "Sophie," she said softly, "remember Jesus."
>
> "Yes," replied Sophie earnestly, almost commandingly, "but you, too."
>
> She left them, her parents, Robert and Magdalene Scholl, with her face still lit by the smile they loved so well and would never see again. She was perfectly composed as she was led away. Robert Mohr (a Gestapo official), who had come out to the prison on business of his own, saw her in her cell immediately afterwards, and she was crying.

It was the first time Robert Mohr had seen her in tears, and she apologized. "I have just said good-bye to my parents," she said. "You understand . . ." She had not cried before her parents. For them she had smiled.[15]

Christoph Probst, the third young man, twenty-three years old, faced death alone. No one in his family knew he was going to die. His wife was in the hospital having just given birth to their third child. After a Catholic priest visited with him to administer the last rites, Christoph said, "Now, my death will be easy and joyful."[16]

The three of them, after being allowed a brief visit, met their death with dignity and victory. Observers commented that Sophie walked to her death without flinching. Hans cried out just before they cut off his head, "Long live freedom!" A single rose was found in his pocket, no doubt as a final statement that what they had done to free Germany would outlive their deaths.

And freedom did prevail in Germany. Hitler committed suicide, and the invincible Third Reich was overthrown. The stalwart stance they took for their beliefs shook a nation and is still impacting lives around the world through print and media today.

Traudl Junge, one of Hitler's private secretaries, spoke with regret of her service to the Nazis when she learned of Sophie Scholl after the war:

> One day I was walking past the memorial in Franz Josef Street to Sophie Scholl, a young girl who opposed Hitler and I realized that she was the same age as me and that she was executed the same year I started working for Hitler. At that moment I really sensed that it was no excuse to be young and that it might have been possible to find out what had been going on.[17]

Standing for Freedom

During the same visit to Germany in which I went to Wittenberg, Reiner told me about the Society of the White Rose. When I heard the story and he suggested that we buy some white roses to give away during the conference at his church, I knew that God wanted us to start a whole new movement of Christian youth who would help reform their nation. The Southstar Church—where our conference was held—is housed in a beautiful old cathedral that used to be Hitler's military chapel. From that chapel, he would challenge his young troops to pledge their lives unto death to him and the Third Reich. After I preached that night about taking up the cause to see abortion overthrown in Germany it seemed only appropriate that we pass out white roses.

So, at the end of the message, I stood and simply said these words while I held up a white rose, "Who will pick up the mantle of Sophie and Hans Scholl and help start a new move of God in this nation?"

It was as if thunder struck in that beautiful old cathedral. While we stood in the same exact place where Hitler called a generation to serve his own blood lust and racist ideologies, a new movement was born. Grown men—affectionately known as "German Oaks" because of their lack of emotion—were surging forward and taking a white rose with tears in their eyes. Younger men and women were no different as they answered the same call.

Sweet justice, don't you think? I wonder if God let the cloud of German witnesses that are in heaven look down from His balcony that night to see what was happening. I believe this reformation will have double the anointing the last one had to reform their nation.

God is looking for more reformers. Are you willing to join us?

Reformer's Prayer

Oh God,
Please use me to change the nations of the earth. Use me
to change and reform my nation. I give myself to you.
In Jesus' name.
Amen.

_____

Signature

_____

Date

---

[1] "Questions & Answers about Germany: Health Care, Health Issues and Social Welfare: Is abortion legal?" *German Embassy Website,*

http://www.germany.info/relaunch/info/facts/facts/questions_en/health/healthissues3.html (accessed: February 23, 2007).

2 "Historical abortion statistics, FR Germany," *Johnston's Archive*, last updated: February 18, 2007, http://www.johnstonsarchive.net/policy/abortion/abfrgermany.html (accessed: February 23, 2007).

3 "German abortion percentages by state, 1999–2004," *Johnston's Archive*, last updated: July 20, 2005, http://www.johnstonsarchive.net/policy/abortion/germany/ab-ges2.html (accessed: February 23, 2007).

4 "Martin Luther: Passionate Reformer," *Christian History & Biography* website, http://www.christianitytoday.com/history/special/131christians/luther.html (accessed: February 26, 2007).

5 Galatians 1:23.

6 For a more complete understanding of the intercessory role in healing nations, please read my book, *Possessing the Gates of the Enemy* (Grand Rapids, MI: Chosen Books, 1994), especially the second chapter.

7 Max Weber, *The Protestant Ethic and the Spirit of Capitalism: and Other Writings*, Translation by Peter Baehr and Godon C. Wells (New York: Penguin Books, 2002).

8 "The White Rose," The Shoah Education Project website, http://www.shoaheducation.com/whiterose.html (accessed March 5, 2007).

9 Annette E. Dumbach and Jud Newborn, *Shattering the German Night: The Story of the White Rose* (New York: Little, Brown, and Company, 1986), quoted in Vicky Knickerbocker, *Study Guide for Sophie Scholl: The Final Days* (Minneapolis: Outreach Coordinator at the Center for Holocaust and Genocide Studies, University of Minnesota, 2006), 4.

10 "The White Rose," *The Shoah Education Project* website.

11 "Battle of Stalingrad," *Wikipedia: the free encyclopedia*, last updated: February 28, 2007, http://en.wikipedia.org/wiki/Battle_of_Stalingrad (accessed February 28, 2007).

12 Society of the White Rose, "Leaflets of the Resistance," The Sixth Leaflet, http://www.jlrweb.com/whiterose/leafsixeng.html (accessed March 1, 2007).

13 Jacob G. Hornberger, "The White Rose: A Lesson in Dissent," Jewish Virtual Library, http://www.jewishvirtuallibrary.org/jsource/Holocaust/rose.html (accessed February 28, 2007).

14 Ibid.

15 Richard Hanser, *A Noble Treason* (New York: G.P. Putnam's Sons, 1979), 279–280.

16 Hornberger, "The White Rose."

17 Traudl Junge, *Blind Spot: Hitler's Secretary*, DVD, directed by André Heller and Othmar Schmiderer (Culver City, CA: Sony Pictures, 2002).

Chapter Ten

Costly Grace

The conflict in Dietrich Bonhoeffer's heart must have been wrenching as he boarded the plane back to Germany from the United States in July of 1939. All his life he had prepared as a theologian, spent his days studying Scripture, and loved God with all his heart.

It had only been one month prior that Dietrich had left his German homeland for America, planning not to return until after the war. What was he doing going back so soon? The Nazis had overtaken his nation and were destroying it with their false ideologies. I can only imagine the various conflicting words of counsel that must have passed through his mind and heart that day. He was just thirty-three years old with his whole life in front of him.

A defining conviction thrust Dietrich toward his destiny as a voice for the salvation of his nation. He wrote to friend and fellow pastor Reinhold Niebuhr before leaving America,

> "I shall have no right to participate in the reconstruction of Christian life in Germany after the war if I do not share the trials of this time with my people. . . . Christians in Germany will face the terrible alternative of either willing the defeat of their nation in order that Christian civilization may survive, or willing the victory of their nation and thereby destroying our civilization. I know which of these alternatives I must choose; but I cannot make this choice in security."[1]

Dietrich came from a long line of those who stood against the status quo for the sake of the kingdom of God. I believe God gives generational blessing and strength that produces a strong legacy for the Lord's purposes at moments of crisis. This was the case with Dietrich Bonhoeffer.

He had already taken to the radio airwaves in 1933 to warn against the dangers of serving an immoral leader. He left the Lutheran church and helped form the Confessing Church in response to the mainline churches' support of the Nazis. This church protested what they called the "Nazified

Pulpit, Nazified Christian Life, and Nazified Clergy." A friend of Bonhoeffer's, Eberhard Bethge, stated it this way:

> We did not interpret our decision as a choice between Christ and Hitler, between the cross and the swastika, and certainly not a decision between democracy and a totalitarian regime. Rather, we understood the issue as one between a biblical Christ and a Teutonic-heroic Christ, between the cross of the gospels and one formed by the swastika.[2]

Turning the Tide of Evil

A close group of friends and family stood with Dietrich against a seemingly impossible tide of evil coming against their nation. Deception as to the true intent of Hitler's policies and programs was rampant, and at that time the world both inside and outside of Germany felt that Hitler could not be stopped.

Being a Bible teacher, part of Bonhoeffer's resistance was to give instruction through God's Word—the truth that sets men and women free. He trained ministers at Finkenwalde. The Nazis declared the seminary illegal in 1937. No wonder Dietrich fled to America to use his gift. However, his catalytic decision to return home formulated from something deep in his heart—he wanted his nation to be free from tyranny.[3]

Less than a year before fleeing to America, he went to see the destruction of German synagogues and Jewish homes and businesses after *Kristallnacht* ("Night of Broken Glass"), November 9–10, 1938. It was a night of riots throughout Germany and in parts of Austria attacking Jews, smashing their shop windows, and burning their holy places. Bonhoeffer went where the violence had been heaviest in Berlin in spite of being forbidden from going there by the Nazis. After this he worked tirelessly to smuggle Jews out of the country.

After his return from the US, Dietrich miraculously got a job as an agent in military intelligence. Through this he was able to travel to try and gain support for the cause to overthrow Hitler's regime. He was part of a botched plot to assassinate Hitler along with a number of other top Nazi officials.

Dietrich was arrested along with his sister Christel and her husband, Hans von Dohnanyi, on April 5, 1943, at the house of his parents. Eventually his brother Klaus and another sister's husband, Rüdiger Schleicher, were arrested as well. At the time of his arrest, Dietrich was engaged to be married, so this must have been especially hard on his fiancé. As it ended, they would never marry.

What Satan meant for evil, God turned for good as Dietrich wrote some 10,000 pages while in prison. His letters were smuggled out through friends and guards. While I do not ascribe to all of his theological points, he's a powerful example of a reformer. While in prison he constantly cheered up fellow prisoners and ministered grace to all he came in contact with—even his jailers. He spent his last days on earth ministering comfort and communion to others.

In the end, Dietrich Bonhoeffer was sentenced to be hung. He was thirty-nine years old. Not only was he executed, but his brother Klaus and his sisters' husbands were as well—a huge blow to the whole family.

April 9, 1945, is a day that will be remembered as a clarion call to resist unrighteousness. That was the day that Dietrich spoke to the witnesses of his execution, "This is the end for me, the beginning of life." The Allies liberated *Flossenburg*, the concentration camp that was his final place of imprisonment, only a few days after his death.

Costly Grace

It has been said that the blood of the martyrs is the seed of the church. Dietrich called what he believed in *costly grace*. In his own words: "*Cheap grace is the deadly enemy of our Church. We are fighting to-day for costly grace.*"[4]

Let me be quick to say that I am not advocating salvation by anything except grace alone. However, since our grace cost Christ everything, we need to be willing to give Him everything for righteousness' sake. Following Christ is costly in terms of reputation, money, time, and how we live our lives. God looked down on the sin of the world and it grieved Him. So it should grieve us to see our society and nation bound with laws and actions that are sinful.

The Visible Church

The role in which Bonhoeffer saw himself stemmed from his belief in the *visible church* as opposed to the church that has nothing to do with what is happening concerning the government and its actions. Historically in the United States, pastors have been very involved in the politics of our nation, even to the point of preaching "election day" sermons. Those who ran for office would come to church to hear what God and the Bible said about the current issues of the day. It was the role of the pastors to keep the nation on a biblical course.

During the American Revolution, pastors even stepped out from behind their pulpits to form what was known as the "black regiment." They were called this because of the black pastoral robes they wore at that time.

Pastors actually led their congregations into battle against what they felt was the unrighteousness of the crown of England. One such pastor was Peter Muhlenberg.

Muhlenberg thought a pastor should not be involved in politics until his brother, Frederick, was driven from his church in New York City by British troops who desecrated the building. He then considered what the Bible says about there being a time for peace and a time for war. (See Ecclesiastes 3:1–11.) After preaching a fiery message with that theme, he cried out, "It's time to fight for those freedoms that we hold so dear. It is time for war!"

I am sure there were gasps from the church members as he proceeded to take off his robes and stand before his congregation in the full uniform of an officer of the Continental militia. He marched to the back of the church, declaring to all, "If you do not choose to be involved, if you do not fight to protect your liberties, there will soon be no liberties to protect!"[5]

Just outside the church army drummers waited. At Pastor Muhlenberg's command, they began to beat out the call for recruits. God's conviction fell on the men of the congregation. One by one they rose from their pews and took their stand with the drummers. Some three hundred men from the church joined their pastor that day to fight for liberty.

I believe that today God is raising up an army all over the body of Christ who will stand against the oppression of biblical truth in their nations. We need pastors and leaders who will "take off their clergy robes"—both in and out of the pulpit—and be a voice for righteousness in the land.

The Rebellion of Disbelief

There have been Christian theologians down through the ages who, rather than help heal their nations, have instead torn down the validity of God's Word as the standard of truth. One was Julius Wellhausen. Before his time there was little doubt in the mind of the general public that the Scripture was the *inerrant*—"free from error"—or absolute truth of God. The Bible was *infallible*—"incapable of erring . . . incapable of failing."

Wellhausen started a whole new line of thinking called "higher criticism." He said that the first five books in the Old Testament were a combination of the work of many authors rather than written by Moses under divine inspiration. Up until that time there was no question that believers—and even nations—could trust the Bible for answers on how we should live our lives. This cracked the bedrock of belief that God is the Creator and Ruler of the universe, and as such deserves to be obeyed. The Bible became just another book. It was no longer considered divine revelation and God's law, but rather a book of good ideas and historical, moral writings.

In the sixteenth century, Luther's rallying cry of "the just shall live by faith" was a high point of Christianity in Germany, but Satan counterattacked with a triple-whammy: Wellhausen's thinking, coupled with the introduction of Darwin's evolutionary theory and Marxism, struck a deep societal blow to the modern world. If the Bible could not be trusted as God's Word and perfect will as Wellhausen's higher criticism proposed, then maybe Darwin was right. If Darwin was right, then maybe there isn't a God at all, and Marx was right that religion (i.e., Christianity) is merely "the opiate of the people."

Sadly, most of the universities, at least in America, that were founded to glorify God such as Harvard, Princeton, and Yale are now bastions of religious liberalism and secular humanism. I have visited campuses where the bells of the chapels that used to peal out an early morning call to prayer are now used for Buddhist meditation. The University of Chicago was founded as a place to train ministers and evangelists. Today the school of divinity teaches world religions and Christianity as just one among many of equal value.

The Great Divide

In America in the 20th century, a great rift developed between liberalism and biblical truth. The liberals (who called themselves "modernists") went with Wellhausen, Darwin, and Marx, cobbling together a religious worldview that eventually denied the fundamentals of historic Christian faith. They wanted the ethics and social justice of Jesus, but they didn't want the doctrine of Christianity.

Meanwhile, evangelical conservatives (whom the liberals call "fundamentalists") held fast to the reformation cry of "the just shall live by faith" and have taken stand after stand for righteousness. However, liberals continued to insist on justice based on social convictions rather than righteousness. While most evangelicals still keep the light of Jesus Christ bright in the area of preaching salvation, sadly, many no longer see it as their Christian duty to extend that saving grace beyond the four walls of their church. For the most part they opted out of the civil rights movement, remained silent about domestic abuse, and rushed to the suburbs.

This void has been filled by feminists founding battered women's clinics and homosexuals who help the poor—now the "good deeds" of our cities are often done by groups that socially and politically stand against what the Word of God says.

Let the Children Come

Perhaps one of the reasons the social service systems of the world are going bankrupt is that the church has given up her role in caring for the poor and needy. Here in the United States, we have something called a foster care program for children from troubled families. At eighteen years of age, these kids are thrust out into the world and out of the program. Usually these children live in as many as five or six homes in their lives, and many are abused in some manner. The church must get involved in these kinds of problems.

Another area the church can help with is adoption. On July 7, 2007, we had a youth prayer day here in the United States, *The Call Nashville*. One speaker talked of our mandate to be willing to adopt children who are unwanted and/or were born to mothers who are involved in drug abuse.

In response, a white couple came forward with a beautiful little girl in their arms. She was around four years old and was of biracial African-American and Caucasian heritage. They told the story of how they had a baby who was stillborn at nine months. They worked for a pro-life clinic and a young mother who decided against aborting her child gave the baby to them instead. Because she had lost her own baby so recently, the adopting mother still had milk to nurse the baby who would have been aborted.

I believe this is a prophetic picture for our generation. God is giving us, His church, the chance to redeem ourselves by rescuing the next generation waiting to be born through our willingness to open our homes and adopt. With all my heart I know that God is going to require members of churches who think that they are beyond the point of wanting to raise a child to be willing to adopt children others planned to abort. We need to prove not only through word, but through deed, that we want to marry righteousness with justice in our land.

This kind of action is costly, but Jesus paid a costly price so that we can obtain grace. We need to really think about the message given to us through Christ's example of "let the little children come to Me" (Matthew 19:14). We need to actively make a difference in our culture. *The Message Bible* says it like this:

So here's what I want you to do, God helping you: Take your everyday, ordinary life—your sleeping, eating, going-to-work, and walking-around life—and place it before God as an offering. Embracing what God does for you is the best thing you can do for him. Don't become so well-adjusted to your culture that you fit into it without even thinking. Instead, fix your attention on God. You'll be changed from the inside out. Readily recognize what he wants from you, and quickly respond to it. Unlike the culture around you, always dragging you down to its level of immaturity, God brings the best out of you, develops well-formed maturity in you.

Romans 12:1–2 THE MESSAGE

Here are some things you can do to make a difference:

1. Ask God who you can personally help.
2. Don't be silent when things are wrong and you see God's laws broken in your culture.
3. The world will try to conform you to its pattern — don't let it!
4. Study God's Word diligently and regularly.

It is critical that we go back to teaching the Word of God in every area of life. We are so influenced by our culture that many Christians don't see anything wrong with exchanging sexual partners. On the university campuses they call it "hooking up" and many times don't even know each other's names. There desperately needs to be teaching to break down the situation ethics that have permeated every part of our lives!

Rather than a social gospel without laws, we need to teach right from wrong and be willing to call sin — sin. Holiness needs to be the theme of the day so the fear of the Lord and the wisdom that comes with it will once again fall on our nations.

There are glimmers of hope all across our university campuses. One of the most exciting of these is the 24/7 movements springing up around the world where young people pray for the sick and release the miraculous on campus after campus. As of this writing, I know of at least sixty college and university campuses with 24/7 prayer taking place in America.

Supernatural Breakthrough

The supernatural breaks down all the natural arguments against God's existence. When you have a terminal illness and God completely heals you, you know that He is real. The power of God breaks down the stronghold of humanism every time. God's power trumps Satan's grip on culture like nothing else will do.

Jaeson Ma writes in his book, *The Blueprint*, of an encounter on the campus of the University of California Los Angeles (UCLA) where a fraternity brother miraculously started walking without his crutches in front of a crowd of onlookers after a group of students prayed for him. Many were weeping at the sight. The healing presence of God was so strong, the people were in awe of God's power that manifested right on the school grounds.[6]

It is important to note here that part of discipling nations includes releasing the supernatural power of God. Remember that the whole commission that Jesus gave us before He ascended into heaven cannot be found in Matthew 28:19–20. The second half of our discipling mission comes through the empowerment given through the Holy Spirit's visitation at Pentecost. Look at how Mark completes the Great Commission in His gospel:

> And He said to them, "Go into all the world and preach the gospel to every creature. He who believes and is baptized will be saved; but he who does not believe will be condemned. And these signs will follow those who believe: In My name they will cast out demons; they will speak with new tongues; they will take up serpents; and if they drink anything deadly, it will by no means hurt them; *they will lay hands on the sick, and they will recover*."
>
> Mark 16:15–18 (emphasis mine)

Signs and wonders bypass the humanist intellect and reveal God in a way nothing else will. When we pray for homosexuals dying with AIDS and they are healed, they will know that the God of the Bible is the real God. Even ardent atheists, when eaten up by cancer, are open to the idea of a loving Savior who will heal their bodies.

If we will only let Him lead us in prayer and pray as He instructs, massive miracles in businesses and schools across the nations will result in Book-of-Acts-type evangelism. If we have nets readied for the harvest through our local congregations, this will result in an enormous multiplication of the kingdom.

My good friend Ed Silvoso points out that the church was added to and multiplied after Pentecost. This resulted in a whole city being filled with the message of Jesus Christ. (See Acts 4:16.) God literally gave us the power to disciple nations through supernatural means. Miracles provide us with a reformational witness of the truth that only Jesus is "the way, the truth, and the life" (John 14:6). We need to be much more proactive in taking miracles to the streets to change our cities for righteousness' sake.

In 1967 America had the "summer of love." People came to San Francisco from all over the world for free sex and drugs. A culture built on drugs was loosed by that generation. Psychedelic music was written under the influence of psychedelic drugs. A few years prior to that time Bob Dylan introduced the Beatles to marijuana in New York City, which started them down a path of drugs and eastern religions.

Around the same time in California there was something called the Jesus movement where many were swept into the kingdom of God.

Thousands were saved during that time, and I was one of them. Young people were baptized in the ocean and people like me were called "Jesus People" or "Jesus Freaks." Our motto was "Jesus is THE WAY." We loved God radically and passionately. However, somehow that move of God never permeated society itself.

Today, we are in the beginning stages of another Jesus movement with evangelism and miracles breaking out on college campuses. It is critical that we mix this fresh move of God with the reformation message and raise up a new generation of voices for righteousness. We desperately need a counter-cultural movement and holy revolution to break with postmodernism.

I want to let you know that while writing this book, as I have typed out line after line, there has been a prayer in my heart:

> Lord, use this book to raise up a new generation of reformers who are counter-cultural. Father God, we need a holy revolutionary people who will be salt and light in their communities and nations! Start a movement of holiness using this book, oh God!

I pray that message is coming through on these pages, not just from what I am writing, but from the working of the Holy Spirit himself—stirring your heart to be a change agent for the kingdom of God.

A New Reformation

Our times require a new reformation—not like the old one that called for the reform of the church only (although there are aspects of the church that still need to become "new wine"), but with societal reformation added to the mix.

Charles Finney, the great lawyer turned revivalist who died in 1875, understood that all aspects of society had to be changed in order for revival to take place. In his book *Freemasonry* he tells about the falseness of this secret order. It is said that he would even have Masons come to the altar and repent of their involvement in the group. This resulted in many of their lodges being closed down.

A former Mason himself, Finney writes of the oath they take in which they swear to what should happen to them if they ever tell any outsider of the secrets of Masonry:

> Binding myself under no less penalty than to have my throat cut across, my tongue torn out by its roots, and my body buried in the rough sands of the sea at low-water mark, where the tide ebbs and flows twice in twenty-four hours.[7]

Finney saw this as no less than idolatrous, and felt it was impossible to be both a Mason and a Christian at the same time.

This great revivalist was not afraid to speak out against evil in the society of his day in spite of possible recriminations. Finney wrote in his book that William Morgan, who was trying to expose Free Masonry, was drowned because he exposed what was happening in secret.

Francis A. Schaeffer says in his book *The Christian Manifesto* that our culture, society, government, and law are in the condition they are in *because the church has forsaken its duty to be the salt of the culture.*[8]

Finney also took a strong stand against slavery as president of Oberlin College. Oberlin was a stop on the underground railroad and a strong warrior in the fight against slavery in our society. In fact, while still a pastor in New York, Finney refused to allow slave owners to take communion because he saw owning slaves as living in sin. Both he and the founder of Wheaton College in Massachussetts, Judge Laban Wheaton, believed in civil disobedience, when necessary, to change a nation.

Civil Disobedience—the Call to Moral Activism

What did they mean by civil disobedience? It meant that when the laws of the nation oppose the laws of God, we ought to obey God and not man. *The Message Bible* puts it like this in Acts 5:29: "It's necessary to obey God rather than men." I like the way that is worded: "It's necessary." It implies that *we have to, we must, we cannot live without or do anything less in our lives than obey God in every part of how we think and act in society.*

What does this mean on a personal level? It means on moral subjects such as abortion, euthanasia, and sexual promiscuity in our entertainment industry, we need to speak out with a loud voice. We need to vote our convictions in national, state, and local elections, speak out for justice and righteousness, and be proactive in every way we can. The bottom line is this:

It is time for moral activism. We ought to obey God and not man. *It is necessary* as Christians to do so.

There are times in the course of our lives when we see an evil and must not only speak out against it, but take some moral action to publicly display our displeasure against it. This is the case for civil disobedience. When we can right a wrong, we need not look for another person to do something—*we* need to do something.

The March on Washington

Civil disobedience has shaped the history of the United States. A young Quaker woman named Alice Paul led one of the first marches on Washington. She was arrested three times, jailed, and went on hunger strikes—all to fight for a constitutional amendment allowing women to vote.

The suffragists marched on Washington to make their point on Inauguration Day, March 3, 1913. The march was remarkably well organized with the colors of the rainbow assigned to women from differing walks of life. For instance, women artists wore shades of red. Wage earners marched together, as did farmers and homemakers. The march was also desegregated, which was unheard of in that day and time. A whole group of African-American women from Howard University in Washington, D.C. marched together as a group and others were dispersed among the crowd.

Finally, on June 4, 1919, congress passed the amendment to grant women the right to vote. It was ratified in 1920, and that year women voted in a presidential election for the first time.

Another famous woman named Rosa Parks refused to go to the back of a bus in Montgomery, Alabama, and went to jail for it. That led to other marches on Washington, D.C. to fight against racism and segregation. The movement was called was called a "moral revolution for jobs and freedom." Probably the most famous speech from these marches took place on August 28, 1963, and was made by a fiery preacher named Martin Luther King, Jr. In it he said:

> I say to you today, my friends, so even though we face the difficulties of today and tomorrow, I still have a dream. It is a dream deeply rooted in the American dream.
>
> I have a dream that one day this nation will rise up and live out the true meaning of its creed: "We hold these truths to be self-evident that all men are created equal." . . .
>
> When we allow freedom to ring, when we let it ring from every village and every hamlet, from every state and every city, we will be able to speed up that day when all of God's children, black men and white men, Jews and Gentiles, Protestants and Catholics, will be able to join hands and sing in the words of the old Negro spiritual, "Free at last! free at last! thank God Almighty, we are free at last!"[9]

Do you have a God-given dream? You can make a change to see God's righteousness and justice released into His world. The call to become a reformer is about living your life each and every day in a way that God's will is done "on earth as it is in heaven."

The great challenge to a humanist-based, liberal society is for Bible-believing citizens to thread their every thought action through the Word of God and see God's miracles and presence again in our midst. Only when we manifest the true love of God in our own lives will those around us understand what they are missing without God's righteousness ruling their lives.

In the United States, Canada, and England, we at least have a memory of what a Christian society should look like, but the memory is fading fast. However, God's light is a bright light. It is stronger and more intense than any darkness Satan can gather. It is time to release that light into our culture again and chase out the darkness!

The Clarion Call

As I am writing the last pages of this book, I must confess that I have been experiencing a swirl of emotions. At times, tears have flowed while I have thought of the enormity of the task at hand to see reformation in our nation. During my research for this book, I happened upon a little book edited by Bramwell Booth, about the life of his mother, Catherine, who founded the Salvation Army with her husband, William.[10] A number of mornings I have crawled out of bed in the wee hours and wept through its pages. One particular passage struck me as I read sketches of her life and quotes of a eulogy written by her husband. These are the words from his lips about his beloved wife, who was struck down by cancer at age 61:

> Lastly, she was a *warrior*. She liked the fight. She was not one who said to others "Go," but "Here let *me* go," and when there was the necessity, she cried "I *will* go!" I never knew her flinch until her poor body compelled her to lay aside.[11]

Cowardice, in her opinion, was one of the commonest and most subtle sins of the day, and she had no patience with those who dared not say, "No," and feared to stand alone.

I have stood at the grave of this "Army Mother" with these and other words from her echoing in my heart. Cowardice? Never! One cannot change a nation from such a stance. She accepted the call of God that not only included the saving of souls, but addressing the social ills of her nation. Can we do any less?

A few years ago some friends and I wrote a document where we repented of the silence of Americans as the holocaust decimated the Jews in Nazi Germany. We presented it along with a wreath at the Holocaust Museum in Washington, D.C. After the presentation, we toured the halls of remembrance together.

As we came to the end of the museum, I stood and read a statement written by Martin Niemoeller, who had been a Lutheran pastor like Dietrich Bonhoeffer in Germany prior to World War II:

> First they came for the Socialists, and I did not speak out--because I was not a Socialist. Then they came for the Trade Unionists, and I did not speak out--because I was not a Trade Unionist. Then they came for the Jews, and I did not speak out--because I was not a Jew. Then they came for me--and there was no one left to speak for me.

After I finished reading this, I stood, transfixed, feeling strongly the Holy Spirit saying, "Don't think this cannot happen in your own nation."

There is a saying that has been attributed to Edmund Burke, "All that is necessary for evil to triumph is for good men to do nothing." This is a time for all of us to do something to change our nations and see that God's will prevails. If not, there may be a day when we are forced to take a stand.

Rod Parsley heard a clarion call in the US and founded The Center for Moral Clarity. In the introduction of his book, *Silent No More,* he writes, "I will be silent no more. I must speak, and I must speak now. Our times demand it. Our history compels it. Our future requires it. And God is watching."[12]

God is watching, indeed. He understands costly grace and wants us as His children to be just like Him. Is there not a just cause? We must answer "yes" in our generation; not only for ourselves, but for our children and those to come. They are counting on us and we must not fail.

---

[1] Dietrich Bonhoeffer *The Cost of Discipleship* (New York, NY Touchstone Publications, 1959,1994), 17–18.

[2] Eberhard Bethge, *Friendship and Resistance: Essays on Dietrich Bonhoeffer,* (Grand Rapids MI: Eerdmans Publishing Company, 1995), 19, in "Review of Eberhard Bethge, Friendship and Resistance," *The Bonhoefferian*, June 16, 2007, http://dietrichbonhoeffer.com/2007/06/18/review-of-eberhard-bethge-friendship-and-resistance/ (accessed September 12, 2007) .

[3] Susan B. Anthony, who was arrested in the United States for voting when it was illegal for women to do so, quoted from the old revolutionary war maxim — *Resistance to tyranny is obedience to God.*

[4] Bonhoeffer, *The Cost of Discipleship*, 43.

[5] Toby Mac and Michael Tait, *Under God,* with Wallbuilders (Bloomington, MN: Bethany House Publishers. 2004), 21.

[6] Jaeson Ma, *The Blueprint* (Ventura, CA: Regal Books, 2007), 174.

[7] Charles G. Finney, *Freemasonry* (Brooklyn, NY: A & B Books Publishers, reprinted 1994), 65.

[8] Francis A. Schaeffer, *A Christian Manifesto* (Wheaton, IL: Crossways Books, 1981), 66.

[9] Lucy G. Barber, *Marching to Washington* (Berkeley: University of California Press, 2002), 170–171.

[10] A special note of thanks to Mary Jo Pierce for giving me this special gift for my birthday one year.

[11] Harold Begbie, *The Life of General William Booth* (New York: The Macmillan Company, 1920), 107.

[12] Rod Parsley, *Silent No More* (Lake Mary, FL: Charisma House, 2005), 1.

Mike & Cindy Jacobs

Don't miss Mike and Cindy's bi-weekly
Podcasts on iTunes.

GENERALS INTERNATIONAL

Please Print

First Name: _____ Last Name: _____

Organization Name: (if applicable) _____

Address: _____ City: _____ State: _____ Zip: _____

Phone: _____ E-mail: _____

☐ I have enclosed a check or money order in the amount of $_____

☐ Please charge to my Credit Card #: _____

Exp: _____ / _____ CVV2# (on back of card) _____   VISA   MasterCard   DISCOVER NOVUS   AMERICAN EXPRESS

Signature: _____

Qty	Item #		Total

Order Total	Shipping Cost		
0-$20	$4	Subtotal	
$20-$40	$6	**Discount Coupon**	
$40-$60	$8		
$60-$80	$10	Shipping	
$80-$100	$12		
$100-$120	15% of ttl	Total Enclosed	

Event code 999⁹

Return to: Generals International PO Box 340 Red Oak, TX 75154 or call (972) 576-8887 x211

Visit us online at www.generals.org